A Child's Book of the Mass

Betsy Puntel and
Hannah Roberts

Illustrated by
Debra Bandelin and Bob Dacey

LTP

LITURGY
TRAINING
PUBLICATIONS

Nihil Obstat
Very Reverend Daniel A. Smilanic, JCD
Vicar for Canonical Services
Archdiocese of Chicago
June 12, 2013

Imprimatur
Reverend Monsignor John F. Canary, STL, DMIN
Vicar General
Archdiocese of Chicago
June 12, 2013

A CHILD'S BOOK OF THE MASS © 2014 Archdiocese of Chicago: Liturgy Training Publications, 3949 South Racine Avenue, Chicago, IL 60609; 1-800-933-1800; orders@ltp.org; fax 1-800-933-7094. All rights reserved. See our website at www.LTP.org.

Illustration by Bandelin-Dacey Studios.

Printed in the United States of America.

17 16 15 14   1 2 3 4

ISBN 978-1-61671-179-5

CBM

For Martha, Ruth, Sarah, Jonah,
Gabriela, Mateo, Ava, Grady, Joel,
and all children

A Note to Parents and Friends of the Child

Surely there is no better way to let children come to know Jesus than to bring them to Mass. Bringing a very young child to Mass each week initiates him or her into the rhythm and spirit of the liturgy and imparts a lifelong love of the Eucharist.

This book is designed to help your child pray the Mass. By focusing on particular moments and gestures of the liturgy, as well as the prayers of the Mass, your child will be able to enter more deeply into this sacred mystery. No one is too young or too little to receive the blessings of the Eucharist.

You can begin by reading the book with your child at home before you go to Mass, perhaps at bedtime the night before. It's not important to read the whole book at once; choose a section each week as a way to become familiar with a new part of the Mass.

Be sure to bring the book to Mass so that you can help your child correlate what is happening in the Mass with the illustrations in the book. Discreetly pointing out and naming what they are seeing assists their participation. When the child is old enough, focus on the questions on each page, which also help your child participate in the liturgy. You may be surprised at how easily and joyfully the child begins to sing and pray with the assembly.

Younger children may need to be held so that they can see what is happening at Mass, or you may want to take that first row seat. Remember that the more the child can see of the Mass, the more engaged he or she will be.

At Baptism your child became a member of the Body of Christ. On that day the Church community promised to support you in raising your child in the faith. We have written this book to follow through on that promise. We hope that your experience attending Mass with your child will be more prayerful and joyful.

Preparing for Mass

On Sunday we go to church to celebrate Mass. We go on Sundays because Easter Sunday is the day when Jesus rose from the dead. Every Sunday is a celebration of the Resurrection.

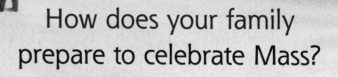

How does your family prepare to celebrate Mass?

The church building is God's house. Church also means God's people. The people of God are the Church, and they are our brothers and sisters in Christ.

What is the name of your church?

When you were baptized, the priest poured holy water over you and said, "I baptize you in the name of the Father, and of the Son, and of the Holy Spirit." When we enter and leave church, we make the Sign of the Cross with the holy water.

Can you find the holy water font near the door of your church?

Can you make the Sign of the Cross?

Before we take our seats, we genuflect toward the tabernacle or the altar. Jesus, the Light of the World, is present in the tabernacle. We genuflect because Jesus is great and we are small. As we bend our knee we give him our love.

Can you find the sanctuary lamp burning near the tabernacle?

Can you genuflect?

Gathering and Beginning of Mass

At the beginning of Mass, the altar servers, lectors, and priest process to the altar. Altar servers carry the cross and candles, and a lector or deacon carries the *Book of the Gospels*. As they process, we sing a hymn. Our voices make a joyful noise to the Lord.

Can you see the cross carried
by the cross-bearer?

Can you see the *Book of the Gospels*
as it is laid on the altar?

Can you join in with the singing?

At Mass, the priest wears special clothes called vestments. The color of the chasubles and stoles changes for different times of the year: in Advent and Lent they are violet in preparation for the great feasts of Christmas and Easter; at Christmas and Easter they are white or gold; on Pentecost Sunday, the great feast of the Holy Spirit, they are red. After Christmas Time and Pentecost they are green for Ordinary Time.

What is the name of your parish priest?

What color chasuble is he wearing today?

What season are we celebrating?

The priest leads us in making the Sign of the Cross, the sign of our salvation. We share this sign from our Baptism. Jesus's Cross is a blessing. We bless ourselves when we make the Sign of the Cross.

Can you see the priest and people make the Sign of the Cross?

At the beginning of Mass we say, "Lord, have mercy. Christ, have mercy. Lord, have mercy." We say we are sorry to Jesus and to each other for the times we have not loved one another as he has loved us. Jesus is always ready to forgive us.

Can you thank Jesus for his mercy and
ask him to help us all begin again
to love one another?

Can you tell him that you need his help
to listen to his voice and follow him?

Lord have mercy.

Christ have mercy.

Kyrie eleison.

Christe eleison.

Now we stand and sing the Gloria. This is the song of the angels. It begins with the words that the angels sang to the poor shepherds in the fields outside Bethlehem on the night that Christ was born.

Can you sing "Glory to God in the highest, and on earth peace to people of good will"?

Liturgy of the Word

During the Liturgy of the Word, God speaks to us through the holy Bible. We ask the Holy Spirit to open our ears and our hearts to hear these words. We try to calm our bodies and be still, to listen. The special place from which the readings are proclaimed is called the ambo.

Can you ask the Holy Spirit to help you listen?

The First Reading is usually from the Old Testament, the first part of the Bible. These are the holy books that we share with the Jewish people, the first people God called to know him. Next we sing a beautiful psalm. The Book of Psalms is also in the Old Testament.

The Second Reading is from the New Testament. It is often from a letter written to the first groups of people who believed in Jesus, 2,000 years ago.

Can you say "Thanks be to God" after the First and Second Readings?

Can you join in singing the psalm?

Next, we sing "Alleluia" as we stand to listen to Jesus's words in the Gospel. The four Gospels in the Bible tell us the story of Jesus's life, Death, and Resurrection. "Gospel" means "Good News." Jesus is Good News for us. Before the Gospel is proclaimed, we make the Sign of the Cross on our foreheads, lips, and hearts. We ask Jesus to place his Word in our minds, on our lips, and in our hearts.

Can you sing the Alleluia?

Can you say "Glory to you, O Lord" before the Gospel?

Can you make the Sign of the Cross on your forehead, lips, and heart?

After the Gospel reading, can you say "Praise to you, Lord Jesus Christ"?

During the Homily, the priest talks to the people about the readings we have just heard. He explains how God is speaking to us today through these readings.

What do you remember from today's readings?

After the Homily, we all stand to say the Creed. In the Creed, we proclaim all the wonderful things we believe about God and the Church.

Can you say some of the Creed?

After the Creed, we pray for the Church, for the needs of the whole world, and for our parish. To each prayer, we respond "Lord, hear our prayer."

Whom did you pray for today?

Liturgy of the Eucharist

After the Prayer of the Faithful, the Liturgy of the Eucharist begins. Eucharist means thanksgiving. This part of the Mass takes place at the altar. At the altar, the risen Jesus gives us his whole self. As we receive this great gift, we become one with Jesus and with one another. This is why we are thankful.

Can you watch carefully what the priest will be doing at the altar?

23

Preparation of the Gifts

The first part of the Liturgy of the Eucharist is the Preparation of the Gifts. The bread and wine are brought to the altar. The bread and wine make us think of God's gifts of creation and the work that people do with their hands.

We also take up a collection for the Church and for the poor. We offer God all our works, and joys, and sad times, too. We offer our money to God.

Can you put your family's offering in the basket?

Can you see how the priest prepares
the gifts of bread and wine?

The priest raises the paten, a plate made of precious metal, with the bread that has been brought to him. Then he prepares the chalice. Into the chalice he pours the wine and adds a few drops of water. The wine represents the divine life that Jesus came to share with us, and the water represents human life. Jesus shared our human life so that we can share his divine life.

Can you see the priest lift up the paten?

Can you see the priest pour wine and water into the chalice?

Next the priest washes his hands. As he washes his hands, the priest asks God to make his heart clean.

Can you see the priest washing his hands?

Can you see the altar servers pouring the water?

Now we stand and sing "Holy, Holy, Holy . . . Hosanna in the highest." On Palm Sunday, crowds of people sang "Hosanna" to Jesus as he entered Jerusalem on a donkey. Now we sing it, with all the angels and saints in heaven, just before the bread and wine become the Body and Blood of Jesus.

Can you join in singing "Hosanna"?

Eucharistic Prayer

After singing "Holy, Holy, Holy . . . Hosanna in the highest," we kneel. The altar reminds us that Jesus gave his life for us. That is why we see the crucifix near the altar. The altar is also the table of the heavenly banquet. The Body and Blood of the risen Jesus will be the food at this heavenly banquet, so we celebrate with lit candles near the altar.

Can you see the crucifix near the altar?

Can you see the candles?

Now the priest asks God the Father to send the Holy Spirit down onto the ordinary bread and wine. The bread and wine will still look and taste ordinary, but they will become the Body and Blood of Christ. We call this moment the "epiclesis."

Can you see the priest's hands extended over the bread and wine?

Through the priest, Jesus speaks the same words that he spoke at the Last Supper, "Take this, all of you, and eat of it, for this is my Body, which will be given up for you." When the priest lifts up the host, it is no longer ordinary bread. It is the Body of the risen Christ.
The priest genuflects, and we can pray in our hearts, "My Lord and My God."

Look! Listen!

Can you see the priest raising the host?

Now the priest speaks Jesus's words as he holds the chalice: "Take this, all of you, and drink from it, for this is the chalice of my Blood, the Blood of the new and eternal covenant, which will be poured out for you and for many for the forgiveness of sins. Do this in memory of me." The priest genuflects and we can thank Jesus who gives us all of himself on the altar.

Look! Listen!

Can you see the priest lifting up the Blood of Christ in the chalice?

We believe that Jesus died and rose from the dead. He will come to us again in glory. This is the Mystery of Faith. At each Mass, Jesus's risen presence on the altar gives us a glimpse of the glory of heaven.

Can you join in proclaiming the Mystery of Faith?

When we eat this Bread
and drink this Cup,
we proclaim your Death,
O Lord,
until you come again.

At the end of the Eucharistic Prayer, the priest lifts up the Body and Blood of the risen Christ and praises God. We respond with "Amen." "Amen" means "Yes."

Can you join in saying or singing Amen?

Communion Rite

Now we stand for the Communion Rite. First, we pray the Our Father. This is the prayer that Jesus taught his disciples, and it is also called the Lord's Prayer. The Our Father is the prayer that Christians all over the world pray.

Can you pray the Our Father?

After the Our Father, we offer the Sign of Peace to our families and church brothers and sisters.

Can you say "Peace be with you" and give a sign of peace to those around you?

The priest breaks the Bread and we pray to Jesus, the Lamb of God, to give us mercy and peace. Like a lamb, Jesus gives his Body to be broken and shared and his Blood to be poured out for us. He invites us to live in peace with God and one another as he gives us the gift of all of himself.

Can you see the priest breaking the Bread?

Can you join in singing or saying
the Lamb of God?

Lamb of God,

    you take away the sins

    of the world,

have mercy on us.

Again, the priest lifts up the host and chalice with the Body and Blood of the risen Christ. He asks us to behold Jesus, the Lamb of God. We respond with a prayer that a centurion said to Jesus, and we ask Jesus to heal us.

Lord, I am not worthy that you should enter under my roof, but only say the word and my soul shall be healed.

Can you ask Jesus to make you ready for the day when you too will be called to receive Holy Communion?

Now is the time of Holy Communion when the people receive the Body and Blood of the risen Christ. You can walk with your parents as they receive Holy Communion. You can invite the Holy Spirit into your heart. The Holy Spirit helps you to be close to Jesus and get ready for the day when you will receive him in the Sacred Bread.

Can you walk with your parents when they go to receive Holy Communion?

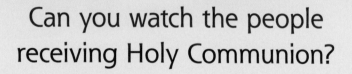

Can you watch the people receiving Holy Communion?

As each person receives Holy Communion the priest or minister of Communion says the words: "The Body of Christ" or "The Blood of Christ."

Can you hear each person respond "Amen" before receiving Holy Communion?

After receiving Holy Communion, we take a few moments to pray silently in our hearts.

Can you feel the silence at this time?

The Mass ends as it began, with the Sign of the Cross. The priest makes the blessing of the cross over all the people, like a shield to protect us. Jesus has blessed you in this Mass.

Can you make the Sign of the Cross?

Can you see the priest and people processing out of church?

The word Mass comes from a Latin word *missa*, which means to send forth. At the end of Mass, everyone is sent forth to love and serve the Lord Jesus. We love Jesus by loving our family, our friends, and the people we meet.

How are you going to
love Jesus this week?